SOCIAL M

CW00499395

MARKETI

Manage your Digital Content and

Social Medias. Learn how to use online

Platforms to canalize traffic and grow

your business thanks to social Media

Marketing

TOM RUELL

Table of Contents

Introduction

Since 2020, companies have basically been forced to take digital marketing seriously with the pandemic. Many companies couldn't rely on foot traffic anymore to generate revenue because of the lockdowns and social distancing. This led to a colossal explosion and demand for digital marketing, and social media is one of the best channels for businesses to leverage. Sprout's Social's 2021 index found that nine out of 10 consumers will buy from brands they follow on social media. 86% will choose that brand over a competitor, and 85% will buy from that brand more often. This means competition is expected to grow, so will consumers' willingness to use this marketing channel to make buying decisions. You can expect social media to get even more competitive over the coming year. As companies start getting better and more competitive in social media marketing, you'll have to compete for attention far more than before. So, here are some things that you can do to compete on a level playing field. Now, a few key factors will differentiate you from your competition. The first one is;

respond to customer service questions promptly. Don't you just hate it when you hit someone up and have issues, and it takes them a few days to get back. You want an answer right then? No one wants to wait, even an hour. Time is everything. Many social media users are engaging with their brands beyond just following up. You need to demonstrate responsiveness and answer the customers in a timely fashion.

Demonstrate an understanding of what they want and need? You should keep customers in mind as you create content because it's all about servicing them and providing stuff for them. It's like I meet some people who are like, oh, I got the best business idea. I'm going to make some cupcakes. Most of the time, I'm like, this is cool, but is there a demand for it? It may taste good, but if there's really not a demand for it, it won't do well. It's not about you and your brand. It's about how you can serve your customers and your audience. Knowing what your potential customers want and need is going to differentiate you from all these brands and other brands that are just churning out content for the sake of highlighting their products, their services, and their own brands. An excellent way to measure this is by looking at different content pieces and seeing which one gets the most engagement. As you discover the types of content that tend to perform well, just do more of them. But here's the thing that no one really talks about in marketing. For those who don't do well, don't do them again. Test them out again once in a while because trends change, and people may like them again. And then, if you do that, you'll keep staying ahead of the curve, and you'll start doing better.

Create more culturally relevant content. Today, we can see more and more brands creating content around cultural events that mobilize people's attention, like Black Lives Matter and the Me-Too movement and even some mainstream sports events like the Olympics. So when you create content around some of these moments and events, especially those you want to support and believe in, no one is doing anything unethical. It's great to keep events, different people, cultures, and genders. And what you want to do is leverage them and show that you're there. And then do not just leverage them to make a financial profit, but also help people. That will resonate with them and create a win-win situation, but you should only do it if you genuinely care. Don't just do something for marketing. Do something because you genuinely care. You should be listening to what's drawing your audience's attention and create content that resonates with those topics. That includes putting out user-generated content because user-generated content is impressive. Also, create educational content about products or services that you're offering.

This is the difference between selling and showing up. Selling is great, but you want to show up and generate sales for yourself. When it comes to your product, It should be about educating and putting things first for others. For example, if you have some fantastic makeup product and your product helps people not just put on the makeup quicker, but just take it off really quick. If you can show how your own product can get off really quickly in one circular wipe, you're going to get sales. You should be able to offer your product in a way that revolves around your customer's problems, needs, and wants, and not just try to sell to them but help them solve those problems. As a product provider, you should actively engage with your clients by responding to their comments questions and even looking at their profiles. This will help you do better.

The Digital Market Sphere

This book will discuss advanced Social Media Marketing and manage your digital content and social media. Gaining tips on how to use online platforms to canalize traffic and grow your business and all of this will be done looking through the lens of social media marketing.

Let us first look at the best digital marketing tools out there, the ones that have gained a solid track record over time, the ones that are popular, and the ones that we foresee as being the go-to tools for the future. So, past, present, and future digital marketing tools are how to look at it.

SEO (Search Engine Optimization)

Search engine optimization or organic search has a mixture of paid and free. Different platforms offer SEO services. Now, let's look into some of these platforms. There's SEMrush. There's also a google free search console. If you don't have an SEO platform, you should look into the google search console. There's also google keyword planner, which is actually situated under google ads and so if you're running google campaigns on google search network or even the display network, you have access to a great tool called keyword planner, and if you know anything about SEO, you'll know that using Google's keyword planner is a good tool. Moz is a freemium tool, meaning they have a free trial that you can sign up for to test drive it, but it's another SEO platform, and it does cost money. These are all surface explanations. Now, let's go forward and dive deeper into SEOs and also try to understand why we use some of these tools.

The first reason would be to find relevant keywords; not only do we want to find relevant keywords, but we also want to find relevant keywords with high volume and low competition, we wouldn't want to find non-relevant keywords with increased competition and low volume, that wouldn't make sense. So, we need a tool to help us put it all together, and the means of choice for this material is Google's keyword planner. It helps us hone in on keywords we may be interested in optimizing, and this is because it is relevant and has a high volume and low competition.

Google Keyword planner

The idea of using Google's keyword planner is one we want to get an idea of what other keywords are out there that are relevant, so it helps stimulate some ideas for relevancy

we can get an average monthly search volume, so we want to know on average over the past 12 months how many search queries you can expect from this keyword and then

You can get a sense of the competition; how competitive is this keyword? So if I try to optimize for this keyword and want to rank for it organically, is it competitive? If it's competitive, it's probably going to take me a bit longer to be found for this keyword on page one of google.

So, that's the whole idea behind Google's keyword planner and note that you could change some of the settings here so if you want to choose a different language, okay you can hone in on a longer or shorter period you can even select a specific location

Moz

Moz has an embedded tool called "keyword explorer." Moz provides us with the volume of users honing a particular keyword, giving us the competition. It also gives us other keywords that we can potentially hone in on.

Moz delivers many other analyses related to the keyword and provides some keyword suggestions. You have to keep in mind that when you optimize, you're optimizing a page for more than one keyword, so you want to be able to have an excellent portfolio of diverse relevant keywords with high search volume and low difficulty, and then you want to be able to identify those keywords that your competitors are ranking.

Google search console

This tool is free and a must; if you're going to work on SEO, you need to be working in the google search console, so the whole key behind the google search console is your website, and you need to get that site verified.

The social media sphere

You know you need to be on social media to implement any social media marketing strategy. YouTube, Facebook, Twitter, Instagram. Some of the most popular sites out there on the web. Even Snapchat. Even though Instagram is crushing it, it's still doing really well. They have over a hundred million active users daily. But as a beginner, all of this is overwhelming and complicated. So how do you start? We will discuss how to get started with social media as a beginner.

The first thing you need to do is pick the right social network. Yes, there's a lot of them. Whether it's Facebook, LinkedIn, or Twitter, it's up to you on which network you want to be on. You could be on all of them, but if you're in all of them, you're not going to spend enough time to make these profiles unique. You don't want half-cooked content on half-baked platforms. In other words, you don't want to be on LinkedIn and do a mediocre job. You don't wanna be on Facebook and do a mediocre job. It's better not to be on them than to do a mediocre job. Because doing a mediocre job will get you no reach, I kid you not. Social media five-six years ago was way easier to leverage to get traffic from. Nowadays, their algorithms are so strict because there's so much competition they're looking for the cream of the crop.

In other words, if you're not the best of the best, you're not going to do well. So you need to pick the right social network. And what's right for me may not be suitable for you. The way you pick the social network is to look up what space you're in. If you're in B2B, the chances are LinkedIn is going to be the best social network for you. Twitter is also another promising social network for B2B, but LinkedIn typically is better. If you're in B2C, Facebook does really well, Instagram does really well, YouTube does really well. Funny enough, YouTube works for both B2B and B2C.

Now here's the thing, you also have to look at what content type you like creating. Are you really good with videos? If so, you probably want to start with YouTube or LinkedIn. Facebook is much more competitive. YouTube, you can get longevity; even if you don't have an audience or have a subscriber pool, you can get more traffic over time. Because Facebook people don't really search on there. YouTube people perform searches all day long for videos, and these contents can continually get views if you rank higher. If you're going after the older demographic, Facebook is fantastic. If you're going after the younger demographic, Instagram and Snapchat are amazing. So now that you have a rough idea of which social network to go after.

Now that you have the right one, the second thing you need to do is start creating content. Yes, you're like, hey, I have no friends and no following. It doesn't matter; no one will follow if you don't have any content. So start creating content. That starts off with completing your profile. Facebook, Twitter, Instagram all of them have profiles. You need to complete everything from a username to your email address to a really proper nice image to a description of who you are or your company. If you don't complete your profile, you're not giving people a reason to follow. And when you're completing your profile, talk about the benefits that people will experience from following you or subscribing to your page. But as I mentioned, it's all about creating content. So it starts with the profile, and then it gets to content.

If you're unsure what content to create, you need to check out your competition. We all have competitors. Even if you're in a new space, let's say you're Uber and revolutionizing the taxi industry where your competition would be the taxi industry. So you look at what your competition is doing on social media. Now I know Uber is already around; they're a multi-billion dollar company. But give me an example of if I was creating uber from day one, that would be my competition. You look at your closest competitors. It could be in direct competition but still your closest competitors. You want to see what content is doing well for them and what contents are not. That'll give you an idea of what you should do more of and what you shouldn't is much of. If you don't know how to create content, it could be as simple as status updates, you pulling out your phone recording a video of yourself. Sharing some links. And if you're not sure what links to share, you can go to _buzzsumo.com_. Type in any keywords from your industry; it'll show you all the popular articles. That shows you what people like on Facebook, Twitter, and social sites, which will give you an idea of what kind of content will resonate with that social network and what doesn't.

Now that you're creating content, the next thing you need to do is build a connection, and you need to build a connection with people; it's a social network. Just because you're on a computer doesn't mean you're not connecting with humans. So make sure you're friending all the people you know, following them. You're engaging, right? You're building connections. So if it's your friend already, like there's someone you know in person, you can just invite them to friend you on Facebook or follow you on Twitter. If it's someone you don't know, you're going to have to work more to build that connection. And here's how you do this. You look for all the people in your space who post status updates. If they have questions respond to them, help them out. If they have articles feel free and share them if you think they're valuable, right? You can repost, re-share, whatever it may be. If other people on these channels' fan pages are related to your industry, even if it's your competitors and they're asking questions, you can respond to them and help them out. That's how you build a connection. Even when you're posting on your own page, when someone responds with a question or a comment, you should acknowledge that they're there. Thank them for leaving a comment.

Respond when they have a question. That's how you engage. And what I found is over time, as you engage, what you'll see is a lot of people will come back over to your site, they'll follow you. You'll engage deeply with them, and they'll become a loyal diehard follower. It's not just about growing your number and having 1,000 followers or 10,000 followers. Which then gets me into my last tip. And the last tip is don't go for follower count. It's all about having valuable connections, personal ones. Because if your first 100 fans or followers aren't that engaged with you, all these social networks have it in their algorithms where they're looking at a percentage. So if you have a million fans, but only 1,000 engage, they're like, " Whoa, this is a terrible engagement rate. We shouldn't show your content to anyone 'cause no one likes it. But if you had a hundred followers and every single one liked it, shared it, and commented, they did all three of those things; social networks like Facebook are going to be like this, this content is impressive; it needs to go viral because everyone loves it. So it's not about having the most amount of fans; it's about having the most amount of engaged fans. If someone's not going to engage, you don't want them. Don't just pay models to talk about you to get more followers. It's about having the most relevant diehard fans.

Don't push people to your business from day one. Within three months or six months, by all means, you can start talking about your business, slowly mentioning it. Try to get people over to your site and us customers. You can do simple things like just sharing a link. But you don't wanna do that from day one. Why would you wanna promote your business when no one's following you? They're not engaged. If you walked up to a random stranger on the street and you said, "Hey, my name is John. "I know that you buy toilet paper "because everyone uses toilet paper. "Would you like to buy my toilet paper?" They're going to be like, "You're crazy, who are you? "We don't want to buy anything for you." You need to build a connection. No one's going to buy from you until you build that relationship. So don't promote your business until three to six months. I'm to the extreme where I like waiting nine months to a year. But again, you can do it within three to six months. You can promote your business instantly if you're doing advertising from day one. But if you're trying to build up everything organically. You can't promote your business from day one.

These are the most common platforms, although there are hundreds of others. When we talk about social media marketing and competition, we will notice that there are many different types of social media platforms, ranging from microblogging to video-sharing platforms like YouTube, networking platforms like LinkedIn, bookmarking sites, and content sharing sites like Reddit and Q&A sites like Quora. Let us now turn our attention to one of the most prominent social media networks, Facebook.

Facebook is evenly matched or say distributed between males and females, so if I'm skewing my target towards the older or younger ones as my target audience, and half as female and half as male, then I know somewhere in there, whomever I'm targeting is going to be on Facebook just based on these numbers here, so your demographic is likely to be on Facebook. Now that Facebook permits video content to upload films all day, you may publish your YouTube videos on Facebook; like most platforms, videos tend to give more interaction in capitalized sectors.

Facebook has an average of (2.27 billion) two-point two seven billion monthly active users. That number is fluctuating since we talk about billions of monthly active users. Up to 88% of all users are on mobile, so what does that tell you? That means you that Facebook has an app and that app is viral; people tend to use the app more than they use the webpage for Facebook, as they do not necessarily need to log on via the internet on their laptops or PC; they go right to the app it's just easier to disseminate information, more accessible to add, friends, comment, respond and so on, it is then no surprise that 88% of all users use mobile now (66%) sixty-six percent of monthly mobile users use Facebook daily, so a lot of recurring users are going back on a day-to-day basis are two-thirds of the whole figure, so it's an addiction, and what Facebook offers is the opportunity to get information from the people you trust, care about and like to work with, you could also share a group with people you have a common interest with, you could also partake in the same organization, maybe have the same scheme, having the same group with the same passion, and that right there is what Facebook is, the commonality it establishes amongst people, and if you build up a network of that commonality, it is going to be addicting to take part in them. Facebook also bridges that gap between distance and sometimes the feeling of knowing that you are part of somebody's life daily by just being on Facebook is also part of what makes it addictive. Thinking further about it from an end user's perspective makes total sense. Now, if you wear your digital marketing thinking hat, you will be seeing this in the light of "Hey, two-thirds of a group of individuals or multiple users utilize it regularly, and there are billions of active users there."

Some of the things done on Facebook are posting polls, putting your Instagram feed in there, adding testimonials, getting creative, taking advantage of everything Facebook has to offer, and being true to yourself. Before you know it, you're going to start building up a community, gaining a reasonable amount of several likes on your business page, as well as some other tips. Now, for Facebook, when it comes to content you want to schedule your content, you don't want to just continue to post back-to-back you want to space your content out and another great advantage to Facebook as I already mentioned about social media marketing that's advertising so Facebook owns Instagram, they have an excellent tool for communicating called Facebook Messenger and so you can advertise leveraging Facebook messages you can leverage Instagram and what you need to do is if you go to Facebook's ad manager and you create a campaign when you go to create a campaign you are going click on placements and depending on what you are trying to do let us just say you are trying to build brand awareness you can actually hone in on you know Facebook you could hone in on Instagram you could do a number of different things within Facebook you have other ads available to you from single image ads to video ads to carousel see you have a lot of options and the most considerable opportunity on Facebook when it comes to advertising is your audience who are you targeting so remember Facebook has old young and everyone in between men and women and so you can specifically target interest you can specifically target gender and age allocation so Facebook really allows you to hone in on who your audience is if you're advertising and so that's the great thing about Facebook they have a lot of users and your you have an opportunity to hone in on a segment of that user base.

Manage your own media

Get educated now; don't get scared here. I'm not saying that you have to go to college and I'm not saying that you have to take my course. Getting educated can mean a variety of different things for different people. Still, I will say that one of the big things that I do see when people come to me to work with me as their coach is that they do not have an in-depth knowledge of what social media management is about. You need to know that it's essential to understand business and the business terms and the business processes. In addition to just knowing how to organically grow something, there are so many different ways to get educated; it doesn't have to be formal education necessarily.

Keep up to date on industry tools and technology;

Whether or not you want to pursue a formal education in marketing, you must keep up with the tools and tricks of the social media trade. Aside from the creative and community engagement aspects of social media, there is a science. To be successful, you must keep up with the analytics side of things and leverage the insights and data you gather to reach a wider audience. The most effective way to accomplish this is to stay current on the best and most popular social media management and social media marketing software options.

Look for social media opportunities wherever you go; Whatever role you are currently in, there is most likely a related opportunity to begin building your social media profile. Consult with your marketing team or company leadership to see if there is a way to promote your company's products or activities on social media. Also, don't be afraid to look for social media opportunities in your personal life. Encouraging your interests on Instagram may not unswervingly lead to your dream job, but it can add value to your resume and professional portfolio by demonstrating your ability to run a successful social media campaign.

Understand that you're constantly being watched; even if you're just operating a personal account, demonstrating a solid voice and consistent posting can help you get a foot in the door. This, however, works both ways. If you use poor judgment on public social media channels, it can and will be used against you.

Never cease to learn and adapt;

MySpace existed ten years ago. Snapchat has become popular in recent years. Because social media channels come and go, staying informed and adaptable is critical. This applies not only to channels but also to marketing disciplines.

You'll almost certainly need to have a thriving social media presence before you can sign up clients. Create accounts on all major social media platforms and become acquainted with blogging, email marketing, search engine optimization, and graphic design. You'll never be able to market for others if you can't market for yourself.

Even the most experienced social media marketing agencies struggle to find clients. Learn where your ideal potential clients spend their online time, distribute great content and start discussions to make money online.

Let's Talk Tips

Let us discuss some social media marketing tips for small businesses. I have outlined in this session how you can get more traffic to your website from social media. I have also outlined in this session how to get more engagement, and I have given a comprehensive explanation on how to get more followers and have also highlighted how to build your brand in a positive light so that people view your brand and then their trust grows in a significant way.

Now, the first thing you need to do is when you're creating your usernames use the same one, if possible, for all platforms; this means your username for Twitter should be the same for Facebook and should be the same for Instagram and Pinterest. If that is done, it'll make it easier for people to find you on social media

Remember to always have "follow" buttons on your website. If you have "follow" buttons on your website, it allows you to get the most followers possible by leveraging social media and leveraging the traffic from your website, and this is because you want to maximize the number of followers you have to get the most traffic.

You want to make a list of your competitors and industry leaders to study their patterns, so when you do this, and you actually study the people that are the best in your industry, you'll notice that you can find patterns in what they're doing you can find consistent things that multiple brands that are leaders in their industry do that you can incorporate into your business. If you go to twitter.com, you can create a list from your profile of profiles that you want to follow and that you want to observe. You should always be learning from the best as you go on. You should always observe who is doing something well that you want to do well to get the best tools and strategies to get you there.

You need to post daily; the more you post, the better in some cases, but you need to post at least once a day on every single platform; that's one thing you cannot afford to not do. You have to post daily; this will ensure an excellent infographic structure or system in place. You don't want to post any more than twice a day on Facebook because the shelf life of a Facebook post is much longer than, say, Pinterest or Twitter; in other words, it stays in the newsfeed longer on Facebook than it does others. All you need to do is understand the psychology behind and the numbers behind posting, how many different times per day, and why it works. Don't over-post and don't under post

Use easy social share buttons for WordPress. This is a plug-in, which applies if you have a WordPress website. If you don't have a

WordPress website, you might find a different alternative. But WordPress has one of those great options that most social media share buttons don't have, as it allows you to follow somebody after you share their content. So, it naturally gets you many more followers from people already sharing stuff you must have posted before.

Use a scheduler like Buffer or HootSuite. Now, HootSuite allows you to put all your private messages from social media in one dashboard so you can view all of them on one screen; it also allows you to automate posting so you can create a schedule and every time you upload a post into that, it will post it on that schedule automatically for you. Buffer does a lot of the same stuff; they don't have the messaging thing, but they also have West branding, so it just kind of depends on what you're looking for; they both have free plans so you could try out any. You might even find a way to use both of them at the same time. You can always use one of two apps to automate social media a little bit and just make it to where you don't have to keep logging back on just to post every single time.

Studying analytics to find popular trends. Here, you're looking for the popularity of posts; you're looking out for indicators of what posts are working and what posts are not. There are actually a lot of great analytic tools for social media because social media is so popular. Keyhole has a great post called the list of the top 25 social media analytics tools. That is going to be a great list that will show you different tools and what they do to give you an idea of what you'll need, but then, because everybody has their own needs, you need to be studying the numbers from social media because if you don't know the numbers, you won't know how to stop doing what's not working and stop wasting your time and you won't know how to build on things that are working because you won't know which ones are. You won't know which posts are getting the most engagement. So, if you have a post that gets you 50 shares and a post that gets zero, you need to stop doing the types of posts that get zero and build on the ones that get 50 shares. You build your brand more over time by working more efficiently, and to work more efficiently, you need analytics.

Show a little humanity and be relatable. The human side of social media is one of the most powerful strategies. Social media will constantly be changing; it will continuously be improving. Different apps will pop up, different services will pop up, but the same principles will apply. Principles like being human on social media and showing that you're not just a robot, you're not just completely automating everything, you're actually caring about what people are interacting with, you care about responding to their messages.

Make your profile look professional and inviting. Showcase your credibility indicators. Things like these can really earn people's trust before they even know who you are. If you prove that you are trustworthy and credible in your industry, they will trust you more and even thank you more. Putting yourself out with strategic details will build trust with people. Share your accomplishments, share your education your certifications and make a professional profile don't look like an amateur

Interact with your followers. You want to interact with your followers. If you do not, it's going to be too one-sided. Engage with people. Show them that you're reading what they're writing. Giving a personal touch on social media does not give the impression that makes them feel that you are a robot and just posting stuff without actually responding to anyone. The whole idea is that you want to respond to people, join chats, ask followers questions, let them know your opinions, retweet them back, and share the post that you think was really intriguing. This kind of action can help build your brand and really make people like you because they'll see that you're actually paying attention to them and giving them respect and attention

Remember, Facebook Loves Facebook. As a small business, you're probably going to have a Facebook page, one of the leading social media platforms out there. If you have a Facebook page. Now, let us talk about some posts on Facebook and how they work. For instance, when you post content, say a video, and upload it directly to Facebook as a Facebook video and not a YouTube video, you will notice that there will be a lot of engagement. If you compare that to content posted as a link to maybe a video on YouTube, it gets a lot less engagement. So, Facebook loves Facebook. They want you to stay on Facebook; they don't want you to go through links or go to other websites; they want you to stay on Facebook as long as possible. So don't share YouTube videos on Facebook; upload the video directly to Facebook. Don't share a lot of links. Share images. Do things that will get engagement but still keep them on Facebook's website.

Put yourself in your follower's shoes. Think about what they are looking at, put yourself in their position; how would you feel if you showed another brand post what you just posted. It is believed that people don't ever think from the other person's perspective. If you did, you might understand some more. If you cannot figure out why they're not engaging with your profile or why they are not following you on social media, then there's a reason for it, there's an excellent reason for it, you have to just figure it out by putting yourself in their shoes. You can even go to a consumer testing website, where you can test websites and social media profiles and products and things like that to figure out what you're doing right and what you're doing wrong and get other people's perspectives. When you post it, look at your own stuff and figure out how you would feel about it if you weren't a part of the company, or just ask your family and friends or ask people you don't know or ask employees what they think.

80% value 20% percent promotions. Keep this in mind; the 80/20 rule is essential for not driving away all your followers. What you do here is; you post value entertaining, educational type stuff 80% of the time, and then you do promotions for your brand 20% of the time if you do promotions for your brand like coupons and sales and all that stuff all the time people are going to get bored. The point is, they don't care about your advertisements unless they already like your brand, so to get people to like your brand, you need to post things like videos, behind-the-scenes photos, educational stuff, quotes, images of some of your employees having a lot of fun with customers. Always provide value with nothing in return and 20% selling or promoting.

Maximize reach with post timings. Your timing needs to be great; you need to keep this in mind all the time. Post at the correct times, on the right platforms. Different platforms require different posting times. For instance, on Facebook, you look at 9 a.m., 1 p.m., and 3 p.m. For Twitter, 12:00 p.m., 3 p.m., 5 & 6 p.m. Wednesday is the best day to post.

Only use platforms that make sense. Just because there are a few dozen social media platforms doesn't mean you should use every one of them. Just because one brand uses it doesn't mean you should. You shouldn't just be a jack of all social media platforms; you should master just those that will get you more business. It will waste time if it doesn't benefit you and your customer base. Don't waste any time. Work as efficiently as possible on social media

Mix up content mediums. In other words, use photos, words, quotes, videos, infographics, questions, polls. There are a lot of different types of posts that you can do. The idea is to master the art of mixing up your content on social media.

People should not be able to predict what you will post next. Keep them on their toes, and keep them wanting more.

Link your website to all your profiles. This is very important because you're not getting all your business just on your social media profiles. Link your website from all your profiles to get more traffic, get more subscribers to your mailing list, and get more customers trying to get quotes and things like that on your website.

Brand your images and your videos. When you post videos and images, which are some of the most popular ways to get more engagement on social media, you'll notice that branding can really help you. Now, for instance, if you're on Facebook and you share a post on Facebook like I highlighted earlier, you don't want to post a lot of links here, and this is because you'll get a minimal amount of reach of your followers as very few of your followers will actually see links that you post on your page, so it's better to post more images.

We have established that Facebook gives more engagement to posts directly on Facebook and gives less attention to links that lead to other websites. If you study Facebook posts very well, you'll notice there's always a trend of images and directly uploaded videos getting more engagement on Facebook than links leading to other websites. Therefore, you want to do those things. But when you share an image, Now, say you share an image, and there's no link to your profile on the image, people are not going to know much about who the post is from, or let's say they share the image or they save it and post it somewhere else, if you have your logo at the bottom, you will get more people visiting without even having to have a direct link. So, just get your brand in front of as many people as possible, and it is also like a sign. If you go down a street and you do not see a sign for a business like a restaurant or something, maybe there's no direct link, then it's just a place, with no direction or information leading to where it is, but when you can see the brand sign up or down the road even before getting to the location of the business, it gives you a sense of direction. It is the same on social media. Your brand allows people on social media to see who it's from the source of the image. It also makes your image look more professional because the logo always looks good. So, when people share your images and share videos without a direct link, make sure you have your logo on it.

Now, you need to know why people actually engage with things on social media. There's a psychology to it, and there are five main reasons people share content on social media. According to neuroscience, they share it to entertain, inspire, or be useful most times. When people share your post instead of just like it, they share it because they want their friends to see it, and if their friends see it, they feel good about being connected to that post. So, make your post shareable. Make it look good when people share it because it's positive, motivating, entertaining, and engaging. Another thing in psychology is; we share to express who we really are. So, if people resonate with something that you post a lot of times, they'll share it. Community to nurture your relationship. So, you could share it to say they might feel like it helps them connect with people or help them develop a connection with their friends that they haven't talked to in a long time. Motivation is another thing. Quotes get shared a lot if there are quotes because they're motivating. The quote motivates them, and this means it might motivate their friends too.

Let us dive deeper into this. Taking more advanced steps forward;

Find out where your ideal clients hang out. Where are they? Are they on Linkedin? If you're selling B to B, I think Linkedin is a compelling platform because many businesses are on Linkedin. If you're selling B to C, business to consumer, then maybe Instagram is the way to go, Facebook is the way to go, or YouTube is the way to go, Snapchat or Twitter. Whatever it is that you choose. But you want to be very, very clear who your ideal customers are. Who are your ideal prospects, and where do they hang out? Where are they out of this vast ocean of the internet and this information highway? Where do they spend their time? Figure out first, where are they hanging out? Find out, where are they?

Secondly, You want to get in front of them; you want to just pick one out of all these platforms. One of the worst things you can do is get on all these platforms. You've got your Twitter, your Facebook, your YouTube, your Instagram, you got your Linkedin, you try to do them all. When you try to do that, you will fail, a hundred percent, because each channel, each platform has its own uniqueness. You need to market to the audience very differently. The way you talk to them is very different. Unless, like me, you've grown to the point where you have a pretty big team to do all these things when you're just getting started. Just pick one. Maybe it's YouTube, Instagram, or Linkedin. Just pick one platform. And you focus on that platform, and you focus on just mastering and understanding that platform. And you learn everything you possibly could about that one platform.

As you do your marketing, you create content, add value, learn, and get feedback on where the strategy is working in the marketplace. Then you can improve from there. Every single course, let's say you want to learn about Instagram, you want to master Instagram, you want to market on Instagram. Get every course that you can. Read every book that you could on just that, on Instagram. And you master that. And implement the ideas. And you go back and implement. You reflect, learn from it, and you implement. That's how you get going with social media marketing. Don't try to do them all, right? Jack of all trades, master of none.

You sell them something. What? That's right. You fucking sell them something. You need to sell something in exchange for money. You can't just have social media following and hope that someday that will turn into money. I have a friend of mine. I won't name any names. She's a top, one of the top ten influencers in Canada, on social media, top ten, like (claps hands) magazines feature her, like top ten in terms of influence. She's broke, making less than $30,000 a year. Looks glamorous; it looks like there are a lot of followers; you can't make money. And when I was talking to her in private, and she was crying, and she's like, "I've been doing this, I've been creating content, and people think I'm so successful. I've got this massive social media following. I can't even pay my rent." I asked when the last time you sold something to your audience was? She said, "Well, I don't want to sell anything to my audience. They would think that I'm a sellout. I don't know if I should sell something. I can't talk about that. I'm gonna lose my audience." That is the wrong attitude. The only purpose of being on social media is to bring in business. Some people use social media for pleasure; I think poor people break people and use social media for pleasure. I use social media for profit. I'm not on social media for pleasure. I am on social media to make a profit, grow my company, and build my brand. That's the only sane reason to be on social media. As a byproduct of that, I get to impact millions of people. But I don't lose focus because I'm using social media as a tool, as a vehicle to grow my company, period, period. So you need to think about that. What is your intent, what is your outcome? You need to be clear that you're out there. You've got to sell them something. If you cannot overcome that, you have a problem with selling. You'll always struggle with making money on social media.

Chapter One
LinkedIn Strategy

Now let us talk LinkedIn. This is a subject matter that I have always loved to write about, and it's one that many of you will be happy to learn from as you go through the material.

Now let's make our knowledge more concrete. You might still feel unsure or uncertain of what to post for your business on LinkedIn. Let us review some top strategies for post types best utilized on LinkedIn. Now LinkedIn is quite different from other platforms, and your ability to see it through this lens goes a long way. Think about it in comparison to other social media platforms out there. Let's compare Facebook, Instagram, and LinkedIn regarding how you post your content. Facebook has an energy that has self-eye focus. We tend to use the word "I did this," "This happened to me," and it has very self-interested energy. And on Instagram, it has that "us-you-energy." When you think about influencers on Instagram, they want you to click on the product. They want you to know what they're up to. LinkedIn has a we-energy. We want to be spoken with. When you're creating posts and content inside LinkedIn, it's a collective team, peer energy voice. So think about your colleagues and your peers and how you would speak with them, and that's the type of energy we want to see in a LinkedIn post

The LinkedIn Strategy

We are going to go over the best LinkedIn marketing strategy. I have strategically outlined an eight-step plan in chronological order and the most important things you need to consider when implementing a LinkedIn marketing strategy. Now, when you first implement a strategy on LinkedIn, the number one question you need to ask yourself is "Who?". Who do you want to reach? Who is your audience?, Who is a potential consumer of your product?. Having answers to these questions will give a deeper insight into the steps we discuss. Now let's talk about these steps.

Know your audience

who is your avatar? What do they look like on surface level? in terms of geographical location, where are they based, what kind of companies do they belong to? is it a solo entrepreneur? is it a fortune 500 company? These questions will reveal a thing that is not just on the surface level; they go in-depth to dig up the emotional level. You need to understand the people you're selling to, what keeps them up at night, what drives them, what they are most afraid of, and what they are trying to achieve? What will that achievement mean for their personal lives? Now you have to focus on two different levels of understanding;

The surface level and then the emotional level. You want to make sure that you do that work before you even look at any social media strategy on any platform. You need to know who you're marketing to; otherwise, all your efforts are going to be void, and it's just going to be luck whether or not it works.

Optimize your profile

When potential clients come to your profile page or are just there to look, your profile answers three questions, which is really important. When a user comes to your LinkedIn profile, they are subconsciously not aware of it, but they're looking to answer three questions to themselves as fast as possible, and those three questions are

Is this a valuable person to me?

Is this person credible? social proof is where that comes in big time

Is interacting with this person valuable and beneficial to me?

Right now, with a timing sense of urgency, you can answer those three questions through how you layout your profile, then you are onto a winner. Your profile doesn't necessarily need to be or look like a CV. It is a landing page. You have a purpose for it. The kind of conversion you want to gain from somebody who goes onto your profile will determine how you'd lay it out. Do you want them to message you? Do you want them to go to your website? Do you want them to read a blog post? you need to set it up in a way that asks for that response

Grow your network.

Now, when you grow your network grows it bearing two different types of people in mind;

Thought leaders. These could be direct competitors. These could be indirect competitors just in a public space you are interested in.

Clients. These are people you see as ideal prospects, people you want to bring into your network so they can be exposed to your content, which I will be shedding more light on as we move on together. This set of people will come to you inbound most often, even when it's not the right time. They might never approach you on their own. If you approach them outbound, they might not convert, but if they do, have it at the back of your mind that that is an ideal kind of client and that they can be pre-qualified to an extent.

You can also grow using the accessible version of LinkedIn, or you can grow using sales navigation which I'll go into a little more as we move on.

Implement a content strategy

This is so important, it used to be a lot easier to grow on LinkedIn as the organic reach used to be insane, but since LinkedIn has advertising capabilities and now to get more and more spread in any platform, usage of ads are the way forward, as it is harder to get organic growth, but it's not impossible. You have to think about who you're creating your content for when it comes to content.

Out-bounding selling

Now let us address the issue of inbound versus outbound. Inbound is people coming to us. This mainly comes from content and word of mouth referrals and stuff like that, and then outbound is when you're going out and chasing that bread, it's that you're going out, you're going to approach that person, it is you reaching out to them the main thing to bear in mind when it comes to outbound is that it is a fast-selling method. This is the future and what everybody is into; personalization, putting the buyer first, the virtual direction in which sales are heading, and more importantly, is set in place. Outbound, you must realize that you anticipate a personalized answer if you deliver a tailored message to a potential customer. You need to genuinely want to connect with them as human beings; you need to constantly give off the energy to treat them as a person, not as a sales opportunity, essential for outbound.

Referral scheme

Now, this is the one you're probably like, oh, I didn't expect you to throw that in there. Many of the people I lectured and taught when I first started giving out relevant and valuable information to business owners with clients always talked about generating new leads generating new businesses. My question has always been, "what about a current business that you have and current opportunities that you maybe haven't explored yet?". You seem to want to knock on different doors and see which ones open. When it comes to referral schemes, are there happy clients? Clients that you currently work with or that you have worked with in the past that you haven't said: "hey, hello, err… I've got my trail of thought that you haven't reached out to, and I just wanted to ask if you know anybody that would actually be a perfect fit for my services". The thing is this, most of the time, happy clients will do this by themselves, but if you haven't asked, then ask them, and even have an incentive to set up a referral scheme where you say, "Oh, to any of you that refer me a client which I end up signing up, I'll give you a 30% commission on the first month of us working together or a 10% recurring commission every single month for as long as they stay". You need to come up with a referral scheme and an incentive, and that will work as an excellent way for current businesses to continue generating new companies in the background while you also work on your outbound marketing strategy. The referral scheme is super important.

Implement CRM (Customer Relationship Management)

You should learn this; you don't have to do it the hard way. It is more straightforward and essential; you pay attention to where the money is coming from and make sure it stays open. You let that client know that "I SEE YOU" to them. It might not look like that, but you know what you are doing and working on when you call and send the emails. Now, if you ignore the implementation of the CRM and stop tracking your customers on both the front end and back end, you will affect inflow. You would begin to see the effect on your money inflow. You would notice that you are not pulling in as much money. So, get a CRM. It doesn't have to be pricey. You can use a spreadsheet. It can be free also as you can use something like pipe-drive, I think zopto is another one, and there are so many options available in the market, so take a look; you could use a spreadsheet at most and track your conversions. If you don't follow them, you cannot optimize, and this right here is the 101. You could also think of it as a scientific experiment.

Split test and optimize

Now, once you've been using one set of messaging or one type of content you want to take a look at your numbers from that, you want to note them down and say, okay, when I send out 100 messages saying this, I get this many acceptances, this many people accept, many people positively respond to me, this amount of people convert into a meeting, and these many people close. Once you have that information, you can say, "Okay, what happens if I change this variable about the messaging "Do the same thing happen? Track the numbers. Where do you see a higher close rate at the back end, and then you can do the same thing for different marketing elements, so you can do that for messaging? You can also do that for content. You could do a split-test video versus a photo. Use split-test photo versus text. You could split-test photo versus carousel, there are so many different ways you can mix and match, and it's kind of like systemic testing if you were doing Facebook ads or like paid traffic. You could do the same thing for your organic marketing methods as well.

The LinkedIn Prospect

Going further, let us begin to dig this up from a different angle. Another solid tip that I can give you to impact your LinkedIn content strategy is that instead of thinking of LinkedIn as a professional place to put content, replace the word professional with leadership. Create a container of leadership voice that is peer-related, and you will have a very successful content strategy. Let's start high-level and think of several content strategy categories that you can lump your content into, and then we'll get into more specifics.

Industry insights.

The best way to think about industry insights is relevant news in your industry, but you share your different opinion as a company or a brand. Another example of an industry insight is all pertinent conferences or Events or podcasts you recently listened to that you're able to share as a post.

Storytelling.

We want to see some behind the scenes of your business, we want to get access to your team and what is happening, and we also love hearing your experiences and stories. Share the action-oriented type of posts, showing the before and after, or a team that is attending a conference.

Be relatable.

What I mean by that is sharing things that are either humorous in ways that we can relate to you through the books you're reading or podcasts you're listening to. We must recognize each category as a human element, which is the most critical takeaway from each category. Your viewers want access to your thoughts and insights on current articles and news. They want access to your team and stories and what is happening, and lessons learned through your business.

The LinkedIn Prospect II

Now, let's share a quick post formula that you can plug all of your LinkedIn content.

"Open up with a hook."

It is a value-based statement and what that means is that the audience knows why this post will matter to them.

Now, the following part of the content formula is the intriguing line. The goal is to get people to click on the *"See More"* button to expand the entire post. In that intriguing line, we want to know the content that can reveal more to spark inquisitiveness in the ears of the user. If you are about to tell us a story, give us something relatable, or give us your insights into a news topic.

The last part of the formula is the juiciest. Give people a call to action. You have earned the right to that call to action. What I mean by that is you've given us the value; you have told us what we are about to get in the intrigue. You deliver it, and then you provide us with something to do. Either that means booking a call or directing people to click on one of the buttons you created above on your company page.

One bonus tip is to use that call to action to match the language you used in the short tagline that you created for your company page. For example, "If you want to check out the full LinkedIn company page and how to create that tagline, we're going to link that in the description below."

LinkedIn Contentology

Now, you have the language you're going to use. You have the categories that work the best and the post formula. So let's get into the content types.

This first content type is something that most people do not think about, but I'm going to give it away to you; commenting. I want to clarify that you can comment in the newsfeed as a company page as your company brand. That is something that many people do not realize and don't take advantage of. The easiest way to engage on the platform and comment is to first reply to comments already happening on your content. The next best place for your company to comment is to engage and respond to people already tagging your brand and your company in their posts. The final easiest way to comment as a brand is to go out in those community hashtags where your content is already trending and continue to pop up and get visibility for your company brand within those three community hashtags generated.

The second content type is "shares." When you share content on LinkedIn, it gets more visibility when you add your own opinion. That is the value that your ideal client wants to follow and engage with on your company page. Another great way to think about LinkedIn content sharing to your company page is to go out and see what your team is creating on their profiles as content. For example, if you have a CEO or even an intern making content on their profile on LinkedIn.

The third one is text-only posts. On LinkedIn, texts are only three lines. The text-only post has five lines, and then you can open up the rest of the post. So that is the only difference I wanted to point out between text-only and all the rest of the posts on LinkedIn. We have an image with a text post, then show authentic photos instead of stock photos. We want to connect with you and your brand, and you should take advantage of that by sharing authentic images with your branding.

External links, news features, blog posts, and YouTube videos are the following content type. LinkedIn is different from other social media sites. They will push content out to external links, and that is a powerful content strategy to drive traffic from your LinkedIn company page to an external source.

The fourth content type is the document feature. This one is relatively new to LinkedIn, and it is powerful. When somebody checks out your past posts, it has its featured newsfeed just for documents. The other unique thing about documents is that they are swipe-able visual files. What that means for you is that it starts to preview the image of the next slide, which creates intrigue for people to want to see what is next. You may see this as a slidable feature or a carousel-type post on other social media platforms. It is the same thing. The most significant difference is that it's uploaded as either a PDF, a word document, or a PowerPoint slide deck.

The fifth content strategy type is video. I get excited about a video because that is the fastest way to connect visually with your customers and get clients. Plus, video on LinkedIn is still undersaturated. Keep the videos short, either a minute to two minutes long, and we want to see that there will be people in this video. We want access to who is behind the scenes working on those products or services, even if it's a product or service. Merge the LinkedIn video with either readable content or captions. That way, we can watch the video on silent, and you can get more attention from your potential customers or clients who may be consuming your video at their place of work.

The sixth "content-type" is LinkedIn live video. The number one thing you want to be aware of with LinkedIn live is that it does require an application to get access and a third-party tool to go live on the platform. You can go live spontaneously. You can schedule your life in advance and go live within an event, which creates a chat feature that allows your audience to connect. When somebody opens up your LinkedIn profile, instead of seeing your LinkedIn banner at the top, they will be able to watch you like a TV screen from your LinkedIn profile. It will be the live video playing there. Since people can land on your profile over and over again, you can create a consistent schedule for your LinkedIn lives and direct them to the same link every single time. As of this recording and depending on your third-party tool, the ability to have your banner image turn into the LinkedIn live video is currently only available on the personal LinkedIn profile, but It is anticipated that it might roll out to the LinkedIn company pages.

The next hot new feature for LinkedIn is LinkedIn polls. It is a great tool to use for audience research and marketing questions. Click to start a post. Hover over the image of a survey. It says Create a poll. You open up with a question, and you have four choices your audience can choose. And the poll duration, you can choose from one day, three days, one week, or two weeks. I recommend that works the best is one week of poll duration. That way, you get people to engage in the conversation in the comments. An excellent strategy for polls is to keep it simple. The best way to keep it simple is to have the question in the text post, a call to action to vote, the same question in the poll, and then give people three options, with the fourth option to be other, comment below.

The eighth "content-type" is articles. It is the only type of content on LinkedIn that encourages you to tweet and share them over to Facebook. The key to getting more visibility on your LinkedIn article is to optimize the image. A LinkedIn article has solid potential, when optimized, to go highly viral outside of LinkedIn, and that is probably the top piece of content that can do that on LinkedIn.

The ninth "content-type" is LinkedIn stories. It is a relatively new feature, and It's mainly accessible from your mobile device. Twenty seconds long, you get three ways to drive traffic from a LinkedIn story.

The first one, just by having a company page. You automatically get swiped up on your LinkedIn company stories no matter how many followers. On your profile, then the swipe-up feature is only available to you if you have 5,000 followers and your Follow button is the primary button instead of Connect. At the bottom of every LinkedIn, the story is to reply to that story. On the company page, you cannot exchange messages through LinkedIn stories.

That's why the second option I'm about to give you is essential for company pages. You want to encourage people to click on the image in the upper left-hand corner, the company logo you have uploaded for your company page. That gives them direct access to open up your profile or company page.

And the final LinkedIn content type is LinkedIn events. The way you get access to it is to go to your home page at the top, where you say Add a post. It has the option to click event. You get access to create an event, either as yourself or as a company page. The most potent parts of LinkedIn events are the cover image and logo that goes with the event. My best tip for you is to show people. If people are speaking at your event, showcase their photos, make sure to highlight those attending your event already as a speaker or attendee. Another business advantage to LinkedIn events is creating an opt-in link when you start the event. Every person registering for a LinkedIn event is also added to your email list. A great way to get the word out about your event is the ability to invite attendees from your current audience. You can also create a filter to invite the specific, ideal client to attend this event.

Now let me give an example of a solid post type that is text-only; that you can make within five minutes that gets excellent engagement and response. Announce to the platform that you're getting more active here on LinkedIn, either as your profile or your company page. Ask for advice for whom you should connect with or follow or engage with on the platform; then, pick hashtags where you think your ideal client is currently pursuing. That is a powerful post for LinkedIn because it encourages tagging and engagement and introduces you to new people you may not have connected with before. All of the content types we just covered can get even more reach when paired with a great hashtag strategy.

Chapter Two
Instagram Marketing

Let us now discuss marketing strategies, concepts, and principles that work for Instagram. Instagram is a social media platform that needs no introduction with nearly 1 billion monthly active users and 500 million daily active users. Instagram is a platform drive with marketing potential; Instagram mobile generates more than 7 billion in revenue, and it is home to more than two million advertisers; not only that, marketing on Instagram has the following advantages. You have increased conversions according to research; more than one-third of the people using the app have used it to purchase products which mean by marketing your products on the app, there's a higher chance of conversion, you also have advanced targeting options, and this is, in fact, thanks to Instagram's parent company Facebook. Instagram has access to just about all advertising features offered by Facebook ads; with this, you can advertise to people based on their age, location, gender interests, and much more; you can also build better brand follower relationships; you can stimulate conversion with your followers and build a connection with them. You'll also get a greater understanding of what your followers like and dislike based on their engagement; this enables you to make the content they enjoy more and increase the chance of converting a user to a consumer.

Instagram marketing.

Now, let's look at how marketing is done on Instagram. Let us start with number one

Your bio is the first thing people notice when they get to your page. That is where customers establish their first impression of your brand; therefore, your bio should contain information, fascinating and engaging. Your bio should include a brief description of your company or product, the sort of material you want to share, brand hashtags, connections to other social media sites, and additional information. Your bio should also include a URL to where you want people to go, whether it's your brand's website or a page for a specific product; track this link as well to see how much traffic it delivers.

Now, when your audience is engaged, a calendar allows you to decide what content, captions, hashtags, and videos go live on what day, date, or time; a consistent post schedule enables you to make the most of Instagram; it will also keep your audience engaged and provide you with access to historical posts.

Now, you can keep track of your postings using content calendars. It will also let you plan and automate the publication of your content. We need to create a content calendar. If you ask anyone who works with social media, one of the most important things they will tell you is to have a content calendar.

Shown below is an example of a template.

Ads options are pretty similar to what you have on Facebook. You can now segment your audience based on their likes, interactions, purchasing patterns, and more; you also have several ad styles to select from, such as story advertising, picture advertisements, video ads, collection ads, and more; and you can also put them up from Facebook ads management. Here's an example of Bodyshop advertising in which they use a single picture ad. The advertisement is effective because of its engaging creative, and appealing ad language, enticing customers to connect with the post and click on the link.

You can get greater reach with ads. Paid ads can enable you to get more followers. Engagement leads and conversions, the caveat here being that you'll need to pay for it too.

Having a visually consistent feed on IG is a process that builds up feedback over time. Instagram is a platform where people gravitate towards aesthetically pleasing content, authentic expressions, and diverse perspectives. The objective is that your feed needs to match your brand's identity and appeal to your industry's audience. What works nowadays are candid shots muted earthly tones with a low-key editing style. Your content must feel down-to-earth and your brand approachable.

Always try to tell a story about whatever content you post. The images, videos, and stories you post must tell stories that captivate your audience and connect with them; this increases the likelihood that they will feel closer to your brand and purchase your products; your captions can tell stories that help your brand appear more human and build deeper connections with your audience. Your content should align with what your audience cares about or solve problems they face. Here's an example of how Patagonia's page talks about forests in America. Their posts tell a different story about a separate issue that affects nature. Their brand on Instagram revolves around bringing awareness to such matters.

Using the right hashtags can make the difference between your posts showing up on the explore tab for everyone to see, and it is getting lost in the sea of content. Your hashtags shouldn't be too generic like new year or hash style since they'll have too much competition; instead, mix up trending. Industry-specific keywords to connect with your follower's research on successful hashtags and limit yourself to less than seven in each post. The more the hashtags in your post, the more likely it seems spammy untargeted, and unprofessional to find out what and how many hashtags your competitors use and how you can do something similar you could also create a hashtag for your brand; these need to be short easily memorable and involve your brand name in some way.

Using UGC or user-generated content allows your followers to become more involved with your brand. You can convert followers into your brand advocates using UGC, regardless of the field your brand belongs to. Here's an example of how Starbucks uses user-generated content and takes advantage of their audience to advertise their products; in this post here, they are attracting customers with an image of happy children dressed in

Taking advantage of video ads, most Instagramers state that users have visited their websites and searched or told a friend after being influenced by posts; even though photo ads are still the more popular form of advertising, video advertisements aren't too far behind there are three key video formats when it comes to Instagram ads single video ads that can create 60-second ads carousels are a combination of images and videos and Instagram stories that enable you to combine images and videos to create visually attractive ads here's an example of the brand pizza 73 using story ads to advertise their pizzas it's successful because you're showing off the product they are promoting with well short videos and captions

Partner up with influencers. Connecting with influencers will enable you to connect with thought leaders within the industry and show off your brand to a larger audience by clicking with them. Your brand will have greater authenticity and authority. Influencers need new tools, resources, and guidance to effectively carry out their role and work together as partners. Consider Micro-influencers as they are more affordable and closer to their audience. We can see how Ralph Lauren has collaborated with an influencer to advertise its products. The influencer showing off the latest ralph Lauren has to offer encourages his interested followers to check out the page and buy something for themselves.

Host contests and giveaways as much as you can. Competitions allow your audience to interact with your business by receiving 3.5 times the number of likes and 64 times the number of comments. You may offer a product or service to increase engagement and brand exposure: planning contests, partnering with brands, Identifying contest rules, and much more. Monitoring the competition and then running it is also very important. You need to track your contest performance and promote the results on other social media platforms.

Using stories and IGTv stories allows you to create a combination of photos and videos that disappear after 24 hours. This, in the long run, can significantly influence your reach and engagement rates, even giving your account the chance to show up in the explore section it can also help make your brand seem more approachable and authentic adding links to the Instagram stories can also help with driving traffic to your website.

Track and learn to identify effective hashtags, visual styles, and the best times to post doing this, and you can develop the best practices for your brand. Social listening and analytics will help you fine-tune your marketing strategy and increase Instagram engagement.

Tools and apps

We also need to understand that growing an Instagram account takes a lot of time and energy, and you might need the help of tools to achieve this. While running Instagram ads and reaching out to influencers is highly effective, there are specific tools that you can use to turbocharge your Instagram account. This book will offer several applications and technologies to supplement your growth plan. You'll discover how to expand your reach, save time, develop a brand look and feel, drive more consumers to your online business, and boost loyalty with your current audience.

Now let us discuss these apps and tools to help you level up your Instagram game and set you apart from the others.

Trufan.

With this app, you can discover highly engaged followers and engage them even further to turn them into brand advocates. Basically, with Trufan, you can strengthen these relationships and encourage them to proactively share about your brand via social and word of mouth. Trufan is more than just an Instagram growth tool, and it's a business growth tool that increases fan loyalty and ambassadorship.

Adobe rush.

Rush allows you to edit your videos directly on your phone. It mimics Adobe premiere if you're familiar with that, but it makes it so much easier. It simplifies the process. So even if you're a beginner, you can create captivating videos super quickly, and they even have to format your videos for stories or feed posts. You also get three video exports to start for free.

Display purposes.

This web-based tool delivers all the details that you need to know regarding Instagram hashtags. One of my favorite things about this tool is seeing related hashtags. If your goal is to grow on Instagram using hashtags, then this tool will help spark some ideas for new hashtags while still ensuring that you're hitting your target audience.

Instagram analytics.

Now the thing is this, you might've overlooked Instagram's in-app analytics, but it is a powerhouse. Basically, at just a glance, you can see who your audience is, what kind of content resonates with them, and you can see your growth over time. Using this tool can better cater to your current and desired audience, setting you up for development. So, for example, if you've identified that most of your audience is based in Brooklyn, you might want to create content that connects with a Brooklyn subculture, which will help you expand your growth within that niche.

Gleam.io.

It is widely known that running contests can grow your Instagram account quickly, and with Gleam, you can run tournaments, track entries, pick winners, showcase user submissions, and a lot more. This tool is super powerful, and it makes entries a lot more seamless than other apps. Seamless entries will result in higher conversions and more followers for your brand.

Big Vu.

If you're a small business owner, you understand the importance of personal connection with your audience on Instagram because it increases engagement. Get on camera and chat with your followers as if they were your friends. It will build community, but not everyone is comfortable; not everyone is a pro when putting yourself online. So that being said, Big VU is a teleprompter app that will help you script and shoot your videos so that you can speak on camera, like a confident pro. It's also going to automatically transcribe your words into captions, which makes your videos more inclusive and more of an engaging experience.

Mention-Lytics

This tool tracks the mentions of your brand so that you can identify where your brand is being mentioned most. You're going to want to use that data to understand what content resonates with people. And then once you have a firm grasp on that, you're going to be able to make more content just like that, to continue the buzz and keep that conversation going. This will help with engagement, help exposure, and help with your follower account.

Canva.

Canva is a free web-based graphic design platform where you can easily layout professional-looking content. You can design with graphics animations, you can create with texts, and you can use your original photos, or you have the option of using stock photography. You don't need a degree in design to use this. And even if you're not a hundred percent comfortable with technology, Canva makes it so easy to communicate product drops visually. Maybe you have some quotes you want to put on your Instagram. You can lay out some company news or sale events. Whatever it is that you're looking for, Canva makes it easy. I would recommend you use this tool where appropriate, though, because when you're on Instagram, most users are looking for organic content. Sometimes when you over-design, this tends to lose engagement, so make sure that you're just saving this tool for infographics, or even if you want to put your logo in your profile picture, this is a fantastic tool for that as well.

HootSuite.

HootSuite is a scheduling tool that takes a lot of that grunt work out of posting to Instagram. Images, videos, and stories can be mailed directly from HootSuite, whether you're on a desktop or whether you're on mobile. On this tool, you can dedicate a few hours a month, at the beginning of the month, to scheduling all your content out at once and then not having to think about doing that later. This tool is excellent for growth because it keeps you on track for posting content consistently. And we all know that consistent material is impressive for growing an Instagram account.

Vsco

Vsco is an app that is best known for its filters. Ten of which are completely free when you download the app. So, if you're looking to tighten up your branding, sticking with one or two Vsco filters and applying that to your entire grid will help you develop your brand, look and feel, and more consistency throughout your grid. Whether your brand aesthetic is grunge or whether you're more of the soft and straightforward type, Vsco can help develop that tone and better relate to your desired audience. Having a consistent brand look and feel will help boost the engagement, and it's going to help boost your follower account when it comes to building a brand Instagram profile.

Prequel.

Let us compare these apps in the same field. The Vsco app also offers filters, but the prequel app is trendier, and they're bolder. These are going to be especially useful if you're appealing to gen Z. So, while prequel is not going to gain you more followers directly, this tool is going to help you send visual cues that you are on-trend, and we've come to learn that visual cues are essential to gen

Z, an audience that is highly literate in visual aesthetic. So, if you're marketing to gen Z, the prequel app can be an excellent tool for you.

Keyhole.

Are you using branded hashtags? If you are a keyhole, you can calculate the ROI of your branded hashtags. And if you're working with influencers, Keyhole will also measure if your influencers have successfully used your branded hashtags. Preview, this feed planning app helps you curate a visually cohesive feed. So, you can move your photos around where they look best, and you can schedule them in time for your brand campaigns. It also helps plan your captions, and you can copy-paste and save hashtags.

Dovetale.

If influencer marketing is part of your growth strategy, Dovetale is a fantastic platform to help you find those niche influencers on Instagram. So, you can search by keyword. You can search by location, engagement rate, and the number of followers with this tool. Dovetale helps ensure that your influencer campaigns show a return on investment by starting with the right fit. Brand collabs manager. Dovetale can tend to be a little pricey, so if you're looking for a budget-friendly alternative, Instagram business and creator accounts now have access to Facebook's brand collabs manager. This platform is designed to make it easy for compatible brands and influencers to find each other and collaborate on campaigns. Brands can look up lists of creators based on their past partner creators who liked their account and set up audience matches.

Insta feed.

If you have website traffic and want to convert those people into Instagram followers, you should check out Insta feed. So, this is a Shopify app that will display your Instagram feed beautifully on your Shopify store. And it also includes a link to allow people to visit your page and follow you right away. It will increase your follower count, especially if you have a busy website already.

TikTok.

TikTok has impressive potential to reach a vast audience. By growing your TikTok account, you can convert these followers into Instagram followers as well. So start by ensuring that your Instagram account is connected to your TikTok profile. If you're interested in seeing how to grow a TikTok account as well, make sure that you're leaving me a comment down below, and if enough of you are interested, I will be more than happy to make a video on that as well. Instagram is a great tool to get people talking about your brand, but if you have a product or a service to sell, you're going to need a platform where customers can go ahead and make those purchases.

Shopify

Shopify is a great place to start. Selling online with your e-commerce website has never been easier. It's never been faster, it's never been more scalable, and setting up your store can be done in a matter of days, all by yourself. You don't need a fancy coder to do the work for you. You can get started with a free 14-day trial, no credit card required, and there's no commitment at all. These free 14 days will give you some time to build a branded personalized e-commerce store so that you can start making money on Instagram.

We could go on and on with the list of tools that can be used to promote whatever you are doing on your platforms, but with these tools also, you can create magic and begin to see a rapid improvement in your brand growth. Most of the time, app trends tend to come and go, so ensure that you remain at it, keep follow-up energy, and keep your ears to the ground to flow with the next big thing.

Chapter Three
The Tik-Tok Prospect

One way or the other, you must have come in contact with this new platform Tik-Tok, but you might be feeling a little bit skeptical. With questions like "How am I going to leverage this platform for business growth?" going through your mind. This session will give a detailed overview and feed your mind with the information it needs. The app downloads surpassed 1.5 billion in 2019, making it the second most downloaded app. Which I think is mind-blowing, and their estimates that by the end of 2020, Tik-Tok will be the number one social media app, crazy, right? We will dive into the demographics, unpack the behind-the-scenes of Tik-Tok and see how businesses can and should leverage this platform for growth. I know the fear that you may have, you may say, there's no way my audience is on Tik-Tok. Let's talk a bit about demographics and decide if this is the right platform for you and your business.

One thing that surprises most business owners to learn is that nearly 30% of Tik-Tok users are over 30. 30% of one billion is a lot. There are currently 150 different countries represented on Tik-Tok. 65% of Tik-Tok users are female. During a recent interview with Tik-Tok Corporate, they confirmed that they're working to get that balance as close to 50/50 as possible. It means that you may see a real surge of athletes in an attempt to win over the males that are still hanging out on Twitter. Tik-Tok is learning your interest, and until you have followed quite a few profiles and engaged with people, it's going to be difficult for Tik-Tok to know what to serve you. However, if you keep engaging with the content you like and skipping the content you don't, you will quickly discover that you have an entirely different experience. In recent years there's been a surge of consumers begging for a natural look at the authentic behind the scenes of brands, celebrities, and businesses. We found that consumers were falling in love with brands all over again. Instead of the perfect photo like Instagram, suddenly you're able to show the culture behind the scenes. Maybe you're super fun, perhaps you're super snarky or skeptical, that can deliver on Tik-Tok, it allows your consumers to say yep, I always knew I liked that brand, and now I understand why. Currently, quite possibly, one of the most extraordinary reasons to use Tik-Tok is that there is unlimited untapped viral potential unlike any other platform right now. Stars are being made overnight, and businesses are blowing up. For me, the first signs of potential virality were this time when a client had about 60 followers on Tik-Tok. She put up a video, and overnight, it reached 9000 views. It opened my own eyes as a content creator to the potential for virality for any business. I wanted to test it in my industry and see how it could work, so we created another video breaking down false beliefs in the marketing industry. What was so crazy was that the video went viral in a week, reaching nearly a million views and generating more YouTube subscribers than we had ever had before, the website traffic and actual sales rivaling these sales that we generate from our Facebook Ad spend every single month.

Now, originally tick-tock started with a lot of very young people like Generation Z or the Generation alpha, and some of their videos were a little bit cringe. Still, now it's growing and expanding as a platform. It's undeniable that there is a lot of marketing potential for businesses, so if you run a business and consider any social media marketing. You're ignoring tick-tock then I think you need to read this session to understand better the potential for tick-tock, how many users it has, and how you could be using Tik-Tok to make more money and a more successful marketing plan going forward in this session, I will break down essentially what Tik-Tok is, and why you might want to use it and how you should expect to use it if you decide to use tick-tock in your marketing plan.

Beginning with "what is tick-tock," it has been named the fastest growing app in 2019. It started three years ago as a musical and has 500 million users as of 2019. It's challenging to acquire a precise figure because it's spreading. According to statistics, tik-tok gained 118 million users in the first quarter of 2019, resulting in a massive shortage of creators. People who start creating on tick-tock draw so much faster than they would on Instagram, Facebook, Twitter, or any other platform that is beginning to get a little more saturated, implying that tick-tock has a lot of growth potential and a large user base. We will get into what kind of businesses should be considering tick-tock. People spend more and more time on this app; it's totally and ravishingly spreading among the younger people and starting to move up. Now, as you'll be getting into using this app, I will make a detailed explanation of how to set it up, but before that, the billion-dollar question is, "what businesses should really be considering tick-tock when you're looking at your marketing plan."

The first and most apparent group would be the influencers or marketers. That is talking about people that are basically just out there, who are just popular based on the kind of content they have been delivering over time, and are making money from sponsored posts, where they're advertising for like makeup, or they're advertising for a watch. Now, because they have grown a considerable influence already, people follow them, and because they have an extensive network, companies will come and say, hey, if you wear our watch, we'll give you, you know, $5,000 or more. Now, just because of the influence they have on a large number of people, they will definitely be great for tick-tock, and that is because they can proliferate, and their audience is all that matters; the size of the audience. It's not so much about the click-through rate and other factors like that for them because over time, it's been realized that one of the significant drawbacks with Tik-Tok right now is it's a little bit tricky to monetize, as you don't have the likes of links and URLs like you have on YouTube. You don't get paid for ads like you would on YouTube. Tic-Tok ads are obviously a compelling way, and it's such a large platform right now you can definitely get a lot of exposure, and the ads are something that you should definitely be considering.

The Four Es

Now, there are four E's that I look at every time I am talking or writing about diving into Tik-Tok marketing strategy, and these Es will be discussed below, but before we do that, I'd like to first deal with some things. Now, if you're still feeling skeptical, head on over to the Tik-Tok app right now and go type in the hashtag for your industry, maybe it's hashtag plumbing, perhaps it's hashtag lead generation, perhaps it's hashtag entrepreneurs or hashtag life insurance and checks it out because if your hashtag is there, there's viability for your business on Tik-Tok. The beautiful thing with Tik-Tok is that it is a closed ecosystem; you can link your profile to your YouTube, drive people to your website, drive them to lead magnets. Another opportunity that is just emerging is *"Tik-Tok Ads."* Let me bring something to your attention. I've had a sneak peek behind the scenes, and the CPMs are juicy, the reach is incredible, and the targeting is improving every day. Now, I plan to answer some of the questions about Tik-Tok: What is the point of being on Tik-Tok?. Let us now proceed to discuss these Es;

Education

Entertainment

Engagement

Emotion

If you can tap into these four Es, you will have your loyal customers saying yes and your new markets and audience reached on Tik-Tok saying yes.

Education

The first step with education is to educate your consumers on this platform. For example, I've seen some videos that say, here is what an adequately laid floor looks like, and they show examples of an excellent base versus the shoddy work from one of their competitors. It's beautiful, and businesses can educate their consumers on what they should be looking for, and in fact, that leaves consumers feeling incredibly empowered and trusting you as the right solution for whatever they need to buy.

Entertainment

Secondly, talk about entertainment. The truth is we all like to be entertained, right? Doesn't matter how introverted you are; something must catch your interest, irrespective of how fun or how non-fun it might seem; you want entertainment one way or the other. Some go to movies, perhaps even Netflix binge each evening, listen there's no shame, but your customers are the same way, who doesn't love watching a great series or a movie that keeps them on the edge of their seat? Tik-Tok is no different; in fact, the average Tik-Tok user is spending 61 minutes per day on the app, and 75% of that time is spent on the For You page searching for new content, new profiles to follow, and that could be your businesses content that they're binging in tonight.

Engagement

Thirdly, Engagement. Everybody loves to find people who are similar to them, so when people are scrolling on Tik-Tok, and they find content that makes them say oh, I thought I was the only one, they're so excited to engage because suddenly you've given them permission to say, I feel the same way, or I'm eager to learn about this. You can create literal engagement bait on Tik-Tok, and audiences are eating it up.

Emotions

Now for the fourth E, and this is, in my opinion, the most powerful is Emotion. When you can start to tap into stories, maybe it's the stories of some of your customers whose lives have been changed by your products, perhaps it's a before-and-after that leaves someone feeling incredibly inspired, maybe it was that mission that your team took to another country to impact the world, and you're able to tell the story making people feel good, making them feel happy, making them feel hopeful. When you can touch on Emotion on Tik-Tok, you'll be amazed to see how audiences spring to life. People love to cry, laugh, laugh, and love to, even as crazy as it sounds, get angry, especially when something goes against their values, and this is the perfect place to connect with them emotionally.

The Tic-Tok prospect

Now there are certain types of businesses that are most prime for Tik-Tok, and those are anything that is B2C, especially E-commerce, physical products, apparel, anything you're selling directly to a consumer is excellent for Tik-Tok, anything that has a beautiful aesthetic. Beauty, food blogging, luxury real estate ready for the Tik-Tok market, and any business that naturally has a hero or a spokesperson for the brand make a lot of sense for them to be on Tik-Tok. Now, as promised, I'm going to blow your mind with several examples of big businesses and small businesses that are absolutely crushing it on Tik-Tok.

First up, we have Chipotle, which launched a campaign on Tik-Tok all about avocados. It

Increased their Guac sales for the following week after their campaign by over 63%.

Next up, we have Calvin Klein. Calvin Klein launched a massive traditional media campaign featuring Justin Bieber in Calvin Klein underwear. When they launched their very first Tik-Tok campaign within 24 hours, they surpassed the total number of engagements of that entire traditional media campaign with just their Tik-Tok meetings alone.

We've all heard the song, Old Town Road by Lil Nas X, ♪ I'm gonna take my horse to the old town road, ♪ ♪ I'm gonna ride till I can't no more. ♪ That song hit peak popularity 100% thanks to Tik-Tok. Before that song's release, Lil Nas X was unheard of in the music industry, and through marketing on Tik-Tok, that song became the number one most streamed single of all time. But let's take it a little more practical because that's a really extreme example of what Tik-Tok marketing can do.

Next up, The Bentist is the famous dentist from West rock Ortho, who grew from one location to three with just Tik-Tok marketing alone. Now there's a hidden gem in Tik-Tok, and that is sponsorships. Many of the influencers on Tik-Tok have never been influencers before, and there's not a going rate for support. In fact, just the other day, I spoke to an influencer who is a famous blogger; she had 160,000 followers on Tik-Tok with millions of views. And I asked her what her going rate was for a sponsored post, and she said $25 per sponsored post. So the ability to partner with influencers in a way that's A, more easily tracked, B, more cost-effective, and C, ultimately potentially able to even go viral, is honestly unmatched by any other platform.

Now Let's begin to discuss how you as a product provider can start to harness the power of the Tok, how you can play in the but league games, talking about how you can find and secure sponsorships with influencers even if you're not on the Tik-Tok platform yourself or as a business.

Step one: You're going to search for a hashtag that your ideal audience might use, and you will find the influencers that are putting out top content within that hashtag. Now here's the beautiful thing, you can go straight to their profile, click through to their Instagram and send them a message on Instagram asking them for their rates. The beautiful thing is, you're gonna find, you may just have better results reach, engagement, and ultimately sales than you ever did on any other platform. Understanding how you can monetize Tik-Tok through sponsorships and finding your dream influencers. These are what you'd be sifting through as we proceed. Now one of the best ways to decide if Tik-Tok is a good investment for you and your business is to spend some time on the app, give it a go, test it out, shoot some videos.

Chapter Four

The Pinterest Prospect

Here we will comprehensively discuss an effective Pinterest marketing strategy for your business. The idea here is to help you as a business owner or a blogger to use Pinterest to grow your business and revenue online. Now we will go over this 10-step system of coming up with a simple yet effective Pinterest marketing strategy that will help you grow on Pinterest and boost the traffic and revenue in your online business.

Now, if you're a business or a blogger, you can use Pinterest like any other social media or search engine to grow your business, and the best way to do this is by setting a clear plan of how you want to use Pinterest strategically, so you never invest your precious time into strategies that don't work or take too much time. First, let us familiarize ourselves with this platform's whole concept. What Pinterest marketing is, why it is essential for your online business.

Pinterest is a social media platform where you can share images you create or find online with other pinners, these images and other visuals are then searchable on the platform which makes it a substantial visual search engine similar like google but just with these images here so if I had to come up with a definition, I would say that Pinterest marketing is how you strategically use Pinterest to grow the traffic to your website and blog and this includes creating your own content, say blog content or products and then create dedicated pinnable images to be pinned so you can share on Pinterest for each of those pieces of content and Pinterest users can then search for these pins and click on them and are led back to your website which grows your traffic so Pinterest marketing includes everything from how you come up with a Pinterest content strategy, how you optimize and grow your account and profile to Pinterest SEO to how to use Pinterest to increase the traffic and revenue in your online business. Now the million-dollar question is, "why is Pinterest marketing important in the first place." Getting people to your website and blog is essential; you want to get as many eyes on your content as possible to build an audience, get comments and replies and maybe make some money with ads or sponsored content. When you're a business, it is essential to get new clients and precisely the right people to your site to make an income, right? And there are many ways to grow traffic online, but talking about Pinterest, this tool in itself has become one of the favorites amongst bloggers. It's so effective that businesses start to jump on as well, and you can now not only promote your website but also your product if you are, for example, an online shop, google, and other strategies can take a long time to see results, but on Pinterest, you can see results fast, and that's why people love it so much Pinterest is easier and faster than other strategies.

The Pinterest Prospect

Now you need to be super clear on why you're on Pinterest, so we're talking about your goals and whom you want to attract. There are over 450 million monthly users on Pinterest right now not every one of these people is going to be a good fit for your brand, so I want you to write down who your ideal customer avatar is your so-called ICA (Ideal Client Avatar) who is your dream reader or customer what age and gender is this person what is this person into? What do they struggle with? Then think about how your blog or business is going to help them. Is your content going to inspire, relate, educate or simply bring some fun into this person's life? How can your products solve this person's problem and make their lives happier or more relaxed?

This exercise will assist you in creating content that attracts the right people to the Pinterest app; you don't want to speak to everyone once you're clear on that, you'll have a super easy time coming up with blog post ideas and product ideas, and you'll also know more about which language you should speak to on your pins or in your pin descriptions to address those people so that you attract the right kind of people from Pinterest to your brand, business, or blog now that you're clear on that

I recommend you start with a new Pinterest business account. A Pinterest business account is free, but it unlocks all kinds of cool features like analytics or claiming your website; you don't want to use your account for your blog or business first of all if you're using Pinterest for business or making money through Pinterest, Pinterest states in their terms of views that you need a business account

Create your Pinterest boards. Your Pinterest boards contain all your pins. You save or pin to your account so you can create a pin, and then you upload it to Pinterest, but before it becomes public to Pinterest users, you need to save it to one of your boards, so boards are like folders on your computer and pins are like the documents you store in them. So, boards are a way of organizing your profile. Now, if you're a business selling ice cream, for example, you could create boards around ice cream flavors or homemade ice cream tutorials; if you're a travel blogger, you could make boards around destinations like countries, for example, Italy, Spain, France, or you could create boards around travel interests say hiking snorkeling paragliding or just hanging at the pool and relaxing.

Come up with your content strategy and plan now; if you're a blogger, you got this covered, but if you're a business, I want you to think about how you can come up with regular weekly content to share on your Pinterest profile. Pinterest wants you to share new inspiring content which will help you attract your audience; this means creating weekly content around your business so yes, start a blog where you share either regular blog posts or your podcast episodes or content from your social media like your videos. Your blog then becomes this place where you regularly share relevant new content in addition to the products you sell that you can share to your Pinterest account; this way, each week, you'll have something new to share with your audience on Pinterest, and you're constantly creating new opportunities for people to find you on Pinterest now yes this is additional work, but it's worth it in the long run.

Create your pins. Pins are images you specifically create for Pinterest that you post to the platform and then lead back to your account. Your pins are how people can find your fantastic profile and products, so this is an essential step. You can create many different pin types; there are regular pen images and video pins, recipe pins, and product pins now; this is where your product and blog contents come in. You are to start creating pins for your existing blog posts every time you make a new piece of content. You should also create pins for your product now. If you are an online shop, you can use free design tools like canvas or tailwind create to input a title, a description, and an image, and the device will come up with hundreds of pen designs in literally minutes. Now, once you've designed your pens, you're going to save them to your board so they become public, and Pinterest distributes them to the Pinterest users. By now, you are already halfway through your Pinterest marketing strategy.

You are learning about Pinterest SEO. Now, SEO stands for Search Engine Optimization. It sounds super complicated, but that is precisely why you are reading this right now: to have a breakdown of every social media jargon you will ever encounter. Currently, there are thousands of pins saved to Pinterest every day, and Pinterest has billions of pins already reserved, so how does Pinterest know which pin is relevant for someone when they are searching. For example, wedding inspiration on Pinterest; is where the Pinterest algorithm comes in. The Pinterest algorithm looks at your profile. It looks at your boards, it seems at your pins and your website, and then analyzes everything to understand what you are all about, then it shows your pins to people who might be interested. Now, you can use Pinterest SEO to optimize your account and pins to help the Pinterest algorithm understand your business or blog even better, and this will help your pins reach more and more people and show up higher in the Pinterest search when someone types in a keyword. I want to enlighten you about how Pinterest SEO works in this SEO strategy. Now, the basics are that you know how to optimize your account, and what's important to consider when you pin to Pinterest is that you see massive success fast.

Use tools and services to automate. On Pinterest, consistency is super important, basically like every other social media, and you want to show up with new content regularly, so you become the go-to person for that topic for your audience. Now, there's so much on Pinterest that you can automate. Automation is excellent on Pinterest, and you can use these tools, and you're still going to see a ton of success. There is a scheduler called tailwind which is used to automate your pinning process on Pinterest fully; all you have to do is upload your pins to tailwind and then set a schedule, and then tailwind automatically posts your pins to Pinterest at the perfect time for your audience while you lay asleep.

Grow your email list. It's essential that you also grow an audience off of Pinterest; yes, your Pinterest followers matter and they are great, but it's like with every social account, it does not belong to you. Sometimes I hear about people whose Pinterest accounts got banned or shut down for legit reasons or not; you don't own your Pinterest account, so you must grow your audience off the platform where you've got the control. So, growing an email list is so important, and an email list is when you set up an account with convert-kit as a separate service. Then you start collecting emails from people who visit your blog or shop over from Pinterest once they're on your email list, you have control over when you send out an email about a new blog post or item in your shop, and then a third business email is also one of the most effective ways on how to make money online. Imagine having a thousand email subscribers, and you just created a brand-new product; this means you can send them an email letting them know about your new offer. Your email will land in their inbox as no third party like Pinterest or an algorithm between you and your audience. An email list is a must for every blogger and business owner, and I recommend you start one as soon as you can if you haven't.

As I get towards dropping my pen, another point to note is the need to develop your online money-making plan. You've built a fantastic website or blog, and your Pinterest account is doing great, bringing all these amazing new people over to your space but now what? How will this make you more money or turn that blog of yours into an actual side hustle or even a full-time income?

There are so many ways how you can make money online. You can sell your products or services, use affiliate marketing to make money with ads, or get brands to sponsor your content. You need to sit and figure out what makes the most sense for your business.

It is also essential to understand that just because you have this account on Pinterest and people click on your website link does not mean you are making money online. If you want to make money online, you still need a business, and you still need to sell something, a product or your service, you need to make offers, you need to be paid for ads running on your site. You want to become crystal clear on what you're selling in your online business and how you're planning on making money. If that's your goal, write it down and become very clear on how you're going to achieve your goal. From here, I want you to analyze and repeat what works for you. Now, you also need to understand that data is so powerful, and once you get into a rhythm of pinning on Pinterest, you'll learn what resonates with your audience and what falls flat, you will see trends and be able to create more and more of what's working, and this right here is how you're going to grow your account fast. Repeat what's repeatedly working; it will build trust with Pinterest and your audience and learn to see what your pinners are struggling with the most and how your blogger products can help them. The longer you analyze and repeat what's working, the better you're going to get at Pinterest marketing; you're going to gain confidence in your Pinterest, and it's going to become second nature. Go into your analytics, develop some benchmarks and numbers you plan to track each month to see your progress in black and white, and then keep working and refining your Pinterest marketing strategy, so you get better and better at it.

Chapter Five
Facebook Marketing

Talking about Facebook marketing, this platform alone has helped people get massive results. Writing about leveraging on Facebook marketing in this time couldn't be more educative or fun. Product providers have been able to reach millions of people, generate millions of websites clicks, and produce millions of sales, all while strictly using Facebook marketing

This session will go over everything you need to know about generating tangible results using Facebook. Now obviously, there are many marketing channels to choose from, you have traditional marketing that plays like magazines, billboards, and cold calling, and then you have digital marketing that plays like blogging, google, and social media, so why Facebook? On the surface, it just looks like a place where people connect with their friends, right, so does it offer any real business value? The truth is, Facebook has two essential elements that allow them to stand out from every other marketing channel in the world and the first one is that they have

A user base of over one billion users and you can reach almost anyone who's in your target market on Facebook.

The ability to hold attention. The average U.S adult spends 38 minutes per day consuming Facebook content, and for context, users spend an average of five seconds looking at a website's written content, and that 38 minutes was just on Facebook that doesn't even account for all their other digital platforms like Instagram.

Facebook Marketing

Now, this session is broken into three parts in the first part. We are going to look at Facebook from the organic side, which is all the free features available to businesses like you in the second part, we are going to look at Facebook from the pay side, which looks at all their paid ad features, and in the third part, we are going to look at the combinations and predictions for Facebook going forward.

Facebook organic marketing

Now, the first thing you need to know is that there's a personal side of Facebook and there's a business side of Facebook the majority of these users only use the private side so that's the typical stuff like creating posts sharing content and talking with friends but there's an entirely different side of Facebook which is the business side so if you own a business or working for a company and you are ready to get started then the first thing you need to do is set up a business manager by going to *business.facebook.com* and create an account from here you can start building your Facebook business assets like your Facebook page, your ad account your catalog pixels and more the main thing that you need to know for organic Facebook marketing is your Facebook page in fact nearly everything you do on Facebook business wise will relate back to your page, because your Facebook page is like your hub it's kind of like your personal website but on Facebook's platform so it's really important that you set your page up for success and you know all the features available to you so let's take a few minutes to look at your Facebook page. Now let us discuss some on-screen features that Facebook offers you as a user.

Facebook organic marketing is free marketing, and who doesn't love free? For example, our YouTube channel as a content creating brand is a part of our organic strategy, and we've gone into this year with the expectation that it's going to take a while before it takes off, which means, in the beginning, you will likely see a slow rise in traffic fans or sales so taking the organic route means you're willing to put in the effort and the time.

Now let us discuss four organic tips starting with tip number one;

Create valuable content. The critical takeaway is to give your audience value and avoid selling. It doesn't matter how great your page looks or how many features your page uses if the content is terrible, remember Facebook is a place where people genuinely go to connect with other people, so if you are interrupting that, you better be bringing in some massive value.

Create valuable native content. Native content is simply content that purely lives on the platform. That is important because Facebook has a complex algorithm that helps determine what content they should show to its users, and we found that Facebook posts with links to other places like blogs will get far less reach. There's a time and a place to promote your site, but remember Facebook's goal is to keep their user's attention, so they don't want you and millions of other companies spamming their users with links because if so, then people will stop using Facebook and that's not what you want, and neither does Facebook which is why you want to create valuable content that makes people want to consume share and discuss with. Speaking of discussions, if you're able to spark a positive debate, that can be a quick hack to get more engagement and more reach; however, I would recommend staying away from political or social issues because that can put you in a compromising position.

Use video content. Facebook's goal is to increase their user's attention their time on the platform, so they've already nailed down native range, and now they're focusing more on video engagement, so if you're creating video content right now, you're going to get a significant boost in the algorithm that means more people will share your content and remember the video needs to be all about your audience and bringing them value now hopefully this can help you create a winning content plan

Community development. If you already have traffic and many fans and you need to promote your Facebook page to them, but if you're starting from scratch, then my biggest recommendation would be to start or join Facebook groups because the Facebook algorithm is significantly diminished in a Facebook group setting so that you can reach many people. When you enter a Facebook group, there are usually some moderation rules which in general, most group owners don't want you to spam their members with your sales or your links, so can you guess the most effective way to leverage a group if you said to provide valuable content then you think right when you give good advice feedback or content in a group setting then people naturally want to learn more about you, and you can position your Facebook group or your Facebook page in a way where people can find those assets and become fans, so that takes care of part one of the sessions which is organic marketing

Facebook Paid Ads

The paid side of Facebook marketing is often referred to as Facebook advertising products, which allows you to grow your content and your audience much faster. The first thing you need to know about Facebook advertising is a Facebook ad account. You can set up a Facebook ad account by logging into your business manager and simply creating an ad account, and again, you can go to business.facebook.com to get started. Now, let's say we want to go after some dog lovers. Here we have the objective, and we want to send traffic to the website. You can select a daily budget or even a lifetime budget, and then you can also pick a start date and an end date which is all optional, then you have the audience. You can choose your specific location and target a particular age group or age range. You can choose from different demographics different interests and behaviors that people put out on Facebook.

Some demographics of dog lovers could be groups and people who are dog lovers, and that would be an interest. You can also go after a demographic such as dog groomers, dog trainers, dog walkers, and dog handlers. Once you can make these demographic specifications, you will start getting suggestions of people who are interested in puppies, people who are dog walkers, people who are just interested in dogs or dog health or dog training, people who have pets at home, people interested in dog behavior pet groomers pet stores. You will be given so many options to choose from, and then you can layer these options by narrowing the audience. If we say we want to target these two interests and want them to match another interest, you have to understand the concept of behavioral strategy. Now, let's just say you know this person is an engaged shopper, and maybe this person also has an anniversary coming up within the next 61 to 90 days. Now, there are so many different options and leverage to pull here, but the point is that it is a very sophisticated targeting system and very powerful, and I highly doubt if you would not find your audience using this system.

You have probably seen ads before, but to ensure that you have every information you will need, you need to know that there are a lot of different formats you can choose from; single images or video images, carousel ads collection ads you can even do slide shows and more. This is where you start communicating the value you give to your audience. By now, looking keenly, you can begin to see some of the power within the Facebook ads manager. Statistics have repeatedly shown that the Facebook ads manager is a compelling platform, but let's remember that it is a pay-to-play platform, and its primary value prompt is giving you the ability to reach people faster, but you have to be willing to pay enough. Now let us further discuss some more tips.

Think with the end in mind; this is from one of my favorite quotes from *Stephen covey,* which reigns true even within Facebook marketing and other warriors you want to know your desired outcome before you start advertising. Is it reach, is it engagement, is it traffic, is its app to be installed? Now, most of our clients are looking for leads or sales, but if you don't have a compulsive deal or a warm audience, you may need to start by building up a fan base. Most people won't buy from you during the first interaction; according to HubSpot, the average number of touchpoints needed to get to a sale is eight, so you may need a combination of posts, emails, website visits, or phone calls before a prospect buys from you and someone who has already started this journey will be considered a part of your warm audience.

Start small: If you're just starting or you have not quite figured out Facebook advertising yet, then you don't need to go out and blow 10 000 a month; instead, I would recommend starting with a modest budget of about 1000 to 1500 per month which should give you enough data quickly to fine-tune your audience, and creative secondly don't start by pitching your most expensive offer instead offer something small you can offer something free like a free guide or exclusive video in exchange for an email address or something smaller. Start with low offers to get the ball rolling and establish some trust. My advice is to take a slow and steady approach when building a new relationship. The only exception to this is if you have an impulsive buy; for example, if you're selling some delicious cookies and as soon as someone sees it, they're tempted to buy, and you definitely should start with your fixed price.

Track everything; The most significant advantage of Facebook and other digital marketing platforms is their ability to measure your results with precision. You can see everything from impressions to the same dollar return that you got on your ads. This means you want to make sure you're installing Facebook pixels on your website that way, you can cookie the visitors that go to your website from Facebook. Then you can track exactly how your visitors engage from Facebook to your website now if you're selling a product on Facebook shopping feature, then this is native, and you can track sales from within Facebook ads manager on your Facebook shopping store of which you need to remember that the more native you can be the better effect that it can have on the algorithm.

Those are my top three tips when it comes to Facebook advertising. Now let's wrap up with the final part three of this session here. We will look at how to keep winning using the above combinations and then make speculations for Facebook marketing moving forward from here. We have established that the best outcome for

Facebook marketing is to use both organic and ads advertising methods. Now, let's take a look at a marketing funnel. We will be using an example of a personal trainer. Now, depending on the product you're selling (personal training), you'll need to provide some great exercise plans and advice as part of your organic approach. The following section is your engagement section; where we want to grow our fans and engagement as much as possible, so we're going to start boosting some of those posts, which is now a part of your paid strategy; these first two phrases go hand in hand because you want to build a sizable audience, so let's say we're going after maybe 25 000 fans now once you get to about 25 000 fans you're ready to start making an offer and since you're. All your lovers have to do is give you their name, their email address, their number and book a time to sign up, and so now you're in the consideration phase of the marketing funnel, and you have their email their number, and you're ready to start selling. That will be your warm audience now that you're ready to start emailing, texting, and calling your prospects to talk about buying your core product, which may be your monthly training services. We've combined organic and paid strategies and completed an entire marketing funnel in this example. Now there are endless ways to incorporate organic and paid strategies; for example, you could create an event, advertise it and then follow it up with social media posts, so the key here is to attempt to meet your customers where they are.

Now, let's go ahead and round off this session with the last thing on my mind: Facebook marketing moving forward and beyond. As you can tell with this material guide, Facebook is a company that is still very aggressive in its platform's growth. Facebook favors brands that favor their users. It's a win-win for everybody, so what are some things that Facebook as a marketing platform is pushing right. As I highlighted earlier, videos are becoming more and more critical, as it helps Facebook increase the time spent on their platform, and I believe that long-form video will have a significant advantage in the algorithm as we advance into coming years. Also, I think you're going to see an explosion of growth with Facebook shops because it keeps users on their platform, and it's native, so don't wait. Go ahead and start using some of these content features and producing long-form videos.

Conclusion

After going over everything that has been said, we can come to a conclusion by summarizing everything into these;

Online presence on social media networks is increasing; social media is becoming more popular. Facebook, Twitter, LinkedIn, and Instagram are all growing in popularity. They are now an excellent way to expand your business's growth. Other social media networks, such as Pinterest, Instagram, and Snapchat, are gaining traction in photo and video content and attracting a more comprehensive range of demographics.

Produce content for each social media platform; Create content for your chosen media network. You cannot post the same content on multiple networks simultaneously. So, when it comes to content writing, be inventive.

Social media is a digital marketing tool for telling stories rather than selling products. You can use it to sell your products directly. However, it is more effective to tell them stories about your products to be more engaged with your content.

More graphic, photo, and video content; Make more graphic images, videos, and photos to engage your customers. When displaying your products in it, the quality should be excellent. To create and share more of this type of content.

Conduct promotional and contest activities; You should hold more contests and promotional activities to gain the attention and participation of your target market. Using various digital tools, you can make these activity announcements more effective.

Contents based on research; The content of your post or image should be based on research. You should understand what you're writing about. When displaying facts and figures or quoting existing information, use accurate facts and figures.

More emphasis on mobile social media; 70% of smartphone users use mobile social apps. As a result, you should concentrate your efforts on mobile social media apps. It is an effective method for gaining more users.

Quick response to comments, complaints, and feedback; social media is now handled by the social media department in many companies. People can inquire about you at any time, and they expect you to respond quickly to their questions, complaints, feedback, and comments. As a result, always respond to them as soon as possible. It will increase your work efficiency.

In today's world, the possibilities for using social media are nearly limitless, and the only limitation is your own imagination. To summarize, you will agree with me that we are in a better position now than we were ten years ago in terms of marketing and placing items in the broader viewing range. The Internet has already changed people's lives, and social media has added to that optimism by making selling and buying faster and more efficient, thus making the jobs of product providers and sellers easier. This will work for those willing to put in the time and effort, and it will be a massive money-making operation.

Printed in Great Britain
by Amazon

15124011R00088